MW00476236

Her Place in These Designs

Her Place in These Designs

Rhina P. Espaillat

Truman State University Press
New Odyssey Series

Published by Truman State University Press, Kirksville, Missouri USA
tsup.truman.edu
© 2008 Rhina P. Espaillat
New Odyssey Series
All rights reserved

Cover image: "Nude Woman," sculpture by Alfred Moskowitz; photo by Philip Moskowitz.

Cover design: Teresa Wheeler
Type: Arno Pro © Adobe Systems Inc.; Myriad Pro © Adobe Systems Inc.
Printed by: Edwards Brothers, Ann Arbor, Michigan USA

Library of Congress Cataloging-in-Publication Data

Espaillat, Rhina P. (Rhina Polonia), 1932–
Her place in these designs / Rhina P. Espaillat.
    p. cm. — (New odyssey series)
  ISBN 978-1-931112-89-5 (pbk. : alk. paper)
  1. Women—poetry. I. Title.
  PS3555.S535H47 2008
  811'.54—dc22

                                                              2008043515

No part of this work may be reproduced or transmitted in any format by any means without written permission from the publisher.

The paper in this publication meets or exceeds the minimum requirements of the American National Standard for Information Sciences—Permanence of Paper for Printed Library Materials, ANSI Z39.48–1992.

For my two grandmothers, Julia and Polincita,
who bequeathed me clear and complementary
notions of my place.

Contents

Acknowledgments

My thanks to the print publications and websites listed below, in which some of the poems in *Her Place in These Designs* have appeared or are scheduled to appear.

Ablemuse.com (My Father's Coins)
American Poets and Poetry (Dinner, Ocala, February 1997; Four Lessons; Lily of the Valley)
Blue Unicorn (Exercise)
bottegheoscure@bottegheoscure.net (In That Old Dream Again)
Christian Science Monitor (Poolside)
Cumberland Poetry Review (The Ball Game: Chichén Itzá; Cleaning Out)
The Dark Horse (Blue Valise; Body's Weight; On the Power of Love to Ennoble the Spirit)
Edge City Review (Grainy Bits; In Eight Degrees; Poem in April; Tantrum)
Ekphrasis (Corot, *Man Scything by a Willow Plot*; Nothing New; On the Ambivalence of Angels; *Paul Helleu Sketching with His Wife,* John Singer Sargent; Pentimento; *Portrait of Don Manuel Osorio de Zúñiga; The Bath,* Mary Cassatt)
Garden Lane (Guidelines; Marine Salvage Museum, Florida)
Gods and Mortals: Modern Poems on Classical Myths (On the Walls)
The Formalist (Contingencies; Triptych)
The Hudson Review (Fractals)
Iambs & Trochees (January '41)
Jewish Women's Literary Annual (As She Tells It; Either/Or; On Schedule; Quiet, Now; September)
Light: A Quarterly of Light Verse (The Poet's Husband Engages in Gourmet Cooking)
Lullwater Review (Leonardo's Metaphor)
The Lyric (Before; Evan, Breathing; Exploratory; In Black and White; Item; She Resists, but Barely; Soldier; Woodchuck)
Margie Review (Parable)
Medicinal Purposes (Crab Poem; Evening News; Squirrel)
The New Press (Keeping Up with the News)

Oberon (Translating)
Orbis (Case Study; Lift-off)
Patchwork of Dreams: Voices from the Heart of the New America
    (Purim Parade; Replay)
Phase & Cycle (At the Nurses' Station)
Pivot (Turning the Begonia)
Poetry (*Find Work*; Vignette)
PoetryPorch.com (Remembering My Parents Remembering Books
    They Read Together)
Rattapallax (On Hearing My Name Pronounced Correctly,
    Unexpectedly, for Once)
The Sow's Ear (Kinderszenen)
Sparrow (Augury; On Rereading a Sonnet Written in 1951)
torhouse.org (In the Diner; On the Impossibility of Translation)
The Undertoad (All Saints' Day; Workshop)
WebDelSol.com (Clara, My Unconceived)

Snaps

Good little girl captured in black and white
in nineteen-thirty-nine, how neatly dressed
you look in your white middy, that old light
flat on your featureless expanse of chest.

And here, a decade on, at seventeen—
nice girl with ankles crossed, hands in your lap's
small bounded nest, gold cross against the clean
sweater—ah, Lana Turner! But perhaps

they knew less than they thought they knew, who thought
they had your number and could quite ordain
your choice of road. The camera that caught
your young, obedient pose noted the strain

behind its ease, surprised a certain look
I don't remember in our common face,
as if a passage in some plain old book
opened into an unexpected place.

Where did you get it, that sharp tilt of jaw,
small thrust of hip and shoulder not in keeping
with Mama's touch that bent you to the law,
to sanctities of custom? Something sleeping

when you were told you would not cross this line
or that, talk back, be anything but good,
risk anything—is flashing me a sign,
across the film of years, that yes, we would.

My Father's Coins

My father's coins: they signal where he never
lived to travel, but perhaps had meant
to go, or longed to go, since duties sever
desire from both fruition and intent.

Look, this is threepence: George the Sixth in profile,
with thistles on the obverse; here, the beak
of Mexico clasping a serpent, guile
seized by winged force; here, *République*

Française haloes a maiden laurel-crowned.
And where's this champion riding, lance in place
for combat, horse's hooves on holy ground
and one proud word, *España*? This stern face

is José Artigas, who fought Spain for Uruguay
and died imprisoned by the French. What thoughts
must have blown through my father's hours, like high
and distant flutes! His careful figures, noughts

rounded Palmer-style, all double-checked,
kept errors out and always reconciled
to the last penny, every sum correct,
expenses paid, frail wife and his one child

provided for. But on the credit side,
what was he left with for his voyages
unmade, unspoken dreams unsatisfied?
A sense of having done it well, and yes,

love, that most fluid currency of all
whose coin is valid everywhere, the stuff
of which real wealth is made. I know he'd call
that true. One wants to think it was enough.

Lares et Penates

I. My Mother's Porcelain

Again this morning, painters in their white
overalls: buckets, brushes, bright good cheer
tucked everywhere like dropcloths. Overnight
the look of somewhere else. No longer here—
their absence ghostlike on the spackled wall—
my mother's porcelain dishes, packed away
in boxes, bubble-papered down the hall
like scruples, like those prayers we seldom say
but learned for good, once only. How the new
seduces with its newness, promise of
unconceived designs! *Discard, undo,*
it whispers, *break those fetters worn for love*
but worn too long; be bold, invent the scene;
look how the morning light falls strange and clean!

II. My Father's Books

I understand them, though, the doomed who stay
where the volcano sputters, or the ground
stirs underfoot like an old dog. *One day,*
and who knows when?—they're told—*You will be found*
among the ashes, under some cracked eave
of tin or mortar. Not that they don't care,
but rather that they do—for what they leave;
what leaving takes them to; if anywhere
becomes them like the known; if what they find
balances what they lose, or brings it back.
My father's books, for instance, which I bind
and mend as best I can: these ragged black
chronicles of imperial Spain, this old
Cervantes that he loved, dull red and gold.

4

Remembering My Parents
Remembering Books They Read Together

Imagine this: a railroad flat three flights
up half-lit stairs above a midtown street
where, decades past, my parents spend their nights
playing seventy-eights in August heat,
or dominoes with some post-dinner guest,
or, best of all—memory's chosen scene—
speaking of books they love: maybe *Beau Geste*
or *Don Quixote, War and Peace.* Between
them, details spin: imaginary places—
or places real enough they'll never see—
illuminate their young, remembered faces
with light enough to light the page for me.
So poor, so much endured as man and wife;
but blessed by this one bond that held for life.

In That Old Dream Again

In that old dream again, safe in the pool
of twilit green gone black, that leafy shade
remembered and unreal, we walked, in cool
night breath fungal and minty. And they made
above me—I was small again—a roof
of their heard laughter; for I could not see,
but sensed them as a fact that needs no proof,
being one of those givens meant to be,
like summer and God's mercy. How I yearned,
waking into their absence, to be there
between them as they moved and never turned
toward me again across the changing air,
as if the dark they chose were the true light,
and morning dropped a veil across my sight.

January '41

When I was young enough to have no fear
of harm from strangers, or the human face,
and had been taught that being good meant clear
answers to one's elders, in a place
of sliding ponds and swings I met a man,
a grownup in pea jacket, with a dark
collar shielding all but a raw span
of nose and lip. Around us, Central Park
sank to late afternoon under bare trees.
Here, little girl, he said, and I turned round
and in an instant learned what the chick sees
when the hawk's shadow stalks it on the ground.
Those six blocks home flew past me, numb and cold
as in a dream through which my body went
unmoving. It was years before I told,
before I knew what harm it was he meant.

On Rereading a Sonnet Written in 1951

It is as if a sketch in a child's hand
bearing the scene all children know—a cow
floating on crayoned green meant to be land—
became the place you could not know till now.
Look, fourteen lines you clothed in fancy dress,
in borrowed images, one day at school.
Silly, yet here and there, how luck may bless
with unsuspecting wit the simplest fool!
The ultimate grief, you wrote—as if you'd known,
who had not learned a thing but by report—
is to discover that one dies … alone.
How odd to be that girl, how long—how short—
the lifetime spent in learning if it's true,
what she suspected, what she somehow knew.

Replay

A dusty courtyard of the inner city:
Sunday, September, nineteen-thirty-nine.
Three seven-year-old girls, huffing and panting,
are taking turns jumping an old clothesline.

A younger neighbor stands by to be invited.
He wears a skullcap, white shirt, black pants, old shoes.
Cathy—our leader, because the rope is hers—
is placid: *We're not supposed to play with Jews.*

I am foreign-born; I don't quite know what Jews are,
and think, in my ignorance, that everybody's friends,
but sense, from the sudden aging of his eyes,
something's been said for which there are no amends.

Dorothy scans the ground—we're in her yard—
and I wonder if there's something I should say;
but what? and to whom? And so I fidget
with the knotted ends of the rope, and he goes away.

And that's all of the story, as it happened.
But in my dream we always call him back
to say the words that heal our common exile
and switch the looming future from its track.

Either/Or

If you listen,
the cries of the drowning
will work on you like axes,
bring you down tumbling;
the anguish of others
will lash you together
into a raft
for the business of rescue.
Adrift in sea-swell
or rotting in shallows
you will mourn for
your own lost seasons,
birdsong, the whisper of leaves.

If you turn away,
if the hum of your own green blood
is louder than cries,
driving you skyward
summer by summer,
then the salt anguish of others
will seep down to your roots.
You will grow twisting
seaward like bent knees,
dreaming of rescues.
Burdened by nests and mosses,
you will strain for
the cries of the drowning, mourning
the raft you did not become.

Grainy Bits

The woman caught in black and white forever
is smiling back from nineteen-sixty-four,
from Mississippi; Chaney, Goodman, Schwerner
are dead. *They came for trouble, got no more*
than they were after, she tells the microphone,
important, righteous in her minute fame.

Old now, does she look back and wish she'd known
better, been better? Or—which is the same—
does she invent good reasons for the face
she wore that day, for better or for worse,
because she wore it?
                     In that other place
of skulls, the train bound rumbling for Auschwitz
is cheered on by the farmer's laugh, his curse
permanent among history's grainy bits.

Parable

You dream a man before you with a stick
tugs at a rope that binds a muzzled bear.
A crowd collects. And though it makes you sick,
now that you've bought a ticket to this fair
you follow too, one with the rubes around
a ring of straw. You join those passive faces
to watch the prod, the dance, without a sound,
as one wretch puts another through its paces.
You dream indignant speeches you would make
if you could speak, dream you could rise and fly
this small-town golgotha, and howl awake—
were you unmuzzled—each indifferent eye,
but for the knotted noose that makes you stand,
your pointed stick, the ticket in your hand.

Evening News

Who's that old man, gaunt
as my village priest?
He saw it happen;
his hands fall and rise
telling the story
like some bleak gospel.

Who's that under the
white sheet, stretched and still
like my dead father,
wheeled in by medics?
Children make faces
as the lens rolls past.

Now, a commotion
and the crowd opens,
necks craning one way:
Who's this in handcuffs,
staring at the ground,
looking like my son?

Keeping Up with the News

In the narrow lexicon of newsprint
you inhabit gray, hugging gray stick legs
with the sticks of your arms, a deeper gray.
Your eyes are two dark wells where flies have come
to drink, your mouth a drooping flower that
mimes death in every language in the world.

Your age doesn't matter, the place, the day
when your heavy gray head will bow at last
on its bony stalk. You have pried me loose
from private bones, out of my cave of skin
and safe particulars. Later I see,
in color, even graver news: You are

not gray at all; the earth is reddish brown
and scrubby bushes stir behind you where
you gesture with slow hands that even now
cast real shadows; you have a name someone
gave you at birth; when you die, it will be
at some second on the clock on my wall.

On Schedule

Minutes before takeoff, did he stand
before the mirror on the men's room wall
and sicken slightly, waver at the thought
of that brown paper parcel he had brought
to slip aboard the plane somehow with all
those tourists bound for pleasure? Did his hand
quiver to hear some stranger's little son
told flight would feel like magic, clouds would sink
below them to the sea, and they would rise
into that other blue? Behind his eyes,
was there a cloud? Afterward, did he think
he had to fly, himself, from what he'd done
or was he certain God—or Truth, or Right—
was the one voice that spoke to him by night?

Purim Parade

Who's this coming now?
Queen Esther in tinsel wig;
two sheiks on skateboards;

Tyrannosaurus
Rex clutching his mother's hand;
Death striding on stilts;

a coven of small
witches shrieking in Spanish;
the Temple Youth Group

twirling gilt batons,
shivering in their red tights;
Saint Benedict's School;

the Emerald Band
elegant in kilts, bagpipes
skirling Hatikvah.

Find Work

I tie my hat—I crease my Shawl—
Life's little duties do—precisely—
As the very least
Were infinite—to me—
                    —Emily Dickinson, #443

My mother's mother, widowed very young
of her first love, and of that love's first fruit,
moved through her father's farm, her country tongue
and country heart anaesthetized and mute
with labor. So her kind was taught to do—
Find work, she would reply to every grief—
and her one dictum, whether false or true,
tolled heavy with her passionate belief.
Widowed again, with children, in her prime,
she spoke so little it was hard to bear
so much composure, such a truce with time
spent in the lifelong practice of despair.
But I recall her floors, scrubbed white as bone,
her dishes, and how painfully they shone.

In Black and White

Before I ever was, they swam this river:
missing now from the view, their voices over
swift icy water sing in me as only
what we have heard of sings, echoing thinly
the rubbed inflections of litany and myth.
Later—the tale goes on—after their bath,
they would dry their long hair under those trees
and dress again, and picnic in the haze
of midafternoon shade. A deeper shade
gathers them homeward now at eventide,
Grandmother's little girls, who fed the chicks
and sewed and milked the cow and trimmed the wicks.

Four Lessons

I. Cat's Cradle

If it comes right, if only for these few
turns our four hands bound in their craft of string
spin to one orbit, what our fingers do—
what Father's mother taught me, a child's thing—
is meant to stay the solitary night
with moments of ephemeral delight.

II. Gardening

Delight she lost while young, Grandfather dead
and handsome in his scalloped silver frame.
He kept his black mustache, she their white bed,
three daughters and two sons, his house, his name,
the garden where her trowel made a sound
like prayer, like love, whispering underground.

III. Solitaire

What turns to us from any ground must mean
to promise some return of what we lose—
red silk begonia piercing soil, red queen
flipped face up from the discard—or we choose
so to believe, or wish we could believe
answers like aces hidden in a sleeve.

IV. Singing

Sleeves rolled to clear the strings of her guitar,
Grandmother plays and sings, low and off-key;
I see her clearly, though her song is far
as any song can go, and memory
labors to resurrect it, to recite
blessings, like her, on what cannot come right.

Clara, My Unconceived

Clara, my unconceived, my childhood's last-
and-never daughter, hostage from the past,
what grief has so disarmed you that both hands
have dropped, inert? I find two rubber bands,
a crochet hook, carefully thread them through
holes that shed scant light on the heart of you,
arm you again to deal with a hard world.

A better mother would have kept you curled,
minutely shod and stockinged, prim in white:
this auburn tangle says all is not right,
as do your naked toes and faded dress.
We have not stayed in touch, and I confess
the fault is mine, who earlier loved you so,
more than half of this century ago.

I did not know your not-quite-father then,
who froze in foxholes in the deep Ardennes
while I did long division, learned to cook
and worked on granny squares with this same hook.
When I named you, I had not chosen other
names for your first and second brother,
who would replace you and absorb my care,
thereafter focused on their skin and hair,
their appetites and baths and morning cries.

Poor Clara, from whose blue, unblinking eyes
I cannot hide the depth of my defection,
what issues you bring up for instrospection!
Would we—this side of birth—have done our nails
together? Shopped the malls for summer sales,

trying on things we never meant to buy?
Would you have whispered stories of this guy
and that, of what was said with words and looks?
Would we have shared our work and traded books?

What's to be done with loves that keep themselves
safe, out of time, like you, on dusty shelves!
Permanent in your absence by those streams
we will not ford again except in dreams,
you lie here in my hand, unformed but whole,
like Sister Ada's rendering of the Soul,
whose vacancy, she said, was all its task.
She didn't tell us why. We didn't ask.

Evan, Breathing

Evan, nine months old, round eyes
still wavering from brown to gray,
interrogates the telephone
without a syllable to say.

His father pleads for us who wait,
eager, invisible, all ears,
two hundred thirty miles behind
the world that Evan sees and hears.

"Say hi to Grandma and Grandpa,"
our firstborn coaxes for our sakes,
as if his love could galvanize
some tenuous wire that absence breaks.

Astronomers who comb the sky
for signs that this or that is true
live on the static of the stars,
and tabulate, and make it do.

Evan, your breath is all we sense,
minutely bridging, puff by puff,
the miles, the days, from there to here.
It isn't much. But it's enough.

Tantrum

Hard little heart closed like your own small fist,
blind as the pit of some green fruit, still sour,
you sulk to punish, knowing you'll be missed
until you have your way, playing at power
you hardly understand yet, but perceive
in action, in your mother's vexed half-smile,
your father's grieved reproof: what you can grieve—
or so innocence says, that looks like guile—
you must be master of. But children grow:
already in your wide, unguarded eyes
that tell more than they want, more than they know,
a troubled softness brims toward mute surprise,
toward judgment, toward a new and nameless ache.
That's how the hardest heart ripens to break.

Lift-off

They may be here now, and still ours, those
children yearning to lift off one last
time—the dust that feeds us, thistle, rose
abandoned, gull's cry lost for good—and cast
perhaps one backward look. Think how the steel
severing them from us will split the skin
of boundless night for them, open and peel
that starry fruit they've sworn to live on, thin
crop of darkest fields. Think, if you dare,
how appetite for home will starve that crew
for some remembered feast of salty air,
flavor of orchard autumns, breath of who
knows what forsaken attic, porch, or bed
in which somebody smiled at what was said.

Poolside

Three rings—red, yellow, green—
navigate, spinning
clockwise and counterclockwise,
intent on winning

this race sponsored by summer's
leaf-heavy wind and shallow
wind-speckled water.
See how they veer and follow

each other's sudden
petal-strewn wake.
The ball—watchful, important—
circles to make

its survey of events,
stern referee
bobbing orange and white:
so much to see,

so much at stake, so much
in all this blue
it hardly knows which way to turn
or what to do.

Woodchuck

Helpless, I watch him clamber up the fence,
balance his lumpy brown marauding weight
and drop onto the lawn, all innocence
and guile. No use shouting him off: too late,
now that he's learned the flavor of those young
tomatoes we will never pick or taste.
All that devoted digging, nicely strung
seedlings watered, nurtured, gone to waste!
I dream the trap, practice to understand—
briefly—the hunter's pleasure in the kill,
the rapture of a shotgun in the hand,
hand raised and trigger squeezed … but never will.
And serves me right, I tell myself, who reap
enough that others sowed but could not keep.

Augury

Late summer grass, made candid by long drought,
in patches only, like suspicions tucked
between green stanzas, whispers it about
that brown is coming, that pale grubs have sucked
juices from shallow roots. Shading away
by almost imperceptible degrees
to yellow intimations of decay,
a dusty green still agitates the breeze,
but higher still, perched on his leafy height,
one mockingbird keeps watch over the town,
slower to sing, now that a change of light
sobers his augur's eye when he peers down:
something not quite the same, if not quite wrong,
that makes him doubt the scene is worth his song.

September

This is the season of the not-quite-over,
of branches green but thinning, fanned away
like fingers a child spreads to look again
after those hide-and-seekers. Light is breaking
where bloom was, folds of the world's body
relearning the horizon, pond's reflection

pondering less. Season made for reflection,
but nothing deep: the geese have not flown over
yet, honking as if signaling the body
to look after itself, to fly away
if it can, or brace for changes. Breaking
with summer custom, windows close again,

silence returns, the neighbor mute again,
waving, smiling through glass. Here's my reflection
in slightly darkened air, the image breaking
in two: one remembering sound, and over
that, another who's glad of silence, of the way
things keep their distance now. Time for the body

to come back home, to reacquaint the body
with its slow unbecoming, take again,
after a summer spent giving away
more than it had, for good. Time for reflection,
the first relieved containment, mulling over
the meaning of this pause, this quiet breaking.

Afterward comes a harder, harsher breaking,
a wave more final that assails the body
like recognition reached over and over:

what was lost once is lost, still and again,
the knowledge persevering, one reflection
inside the next, unchanged, moving away.

But while this kindly season has its way,
there's nothing but a cloud of starlings breaking,
wheeling, reforming overhead, reflections
making deep the shallow pond, the body
pretending it, too, has seasons, may again
leaf to begin familiar cycles over.

Better this way. Better to let the body
ease into breaking, seem to stir again,
avoid reflection, forget how much is over.

Before

Heavy with waiting, trees
have ceased to stir at all,
dense with dark auguries,
rain still to fall.

Windless and swollen, tense,
no hum of bees, no birds,
a silence like the silence
before hard words

not to be turned, made right,
said softly, taken back
after the whip of light
and thunder's crack.

Cycles

Leaf by green leaf the ground became the sky
from April to September, straining high
through bole to crown up to the seagull's cry.

With gravity suspended by decree
of some unknown, capricious deity,
a kind of levitation lifted me

all topsy-turvy off my mortal feet,
like hawthorn and white birch and bittersweet.
Or seemed to, rather, since no way to cheat

time or the laws of physics has been found.
October's come: look how, without a sound,
leaf by gold leaf the sky becomes the ground.

Turning the Begonia

I turn it a half-circle: each round leaf
has a new scene to witness in its brief
passage from pursed green to browns and yellows.

Some nod in window drafts, as if their fellows
had whispered clever comments on the view;
some hide behind their elders; one or two
stare at this local sun they did not know,
as if to learn, by watching, how we grow.

Those others, turned outdoors, pressed to the glass,
watch maples toss their dense and writhing mass
and wonder at the silver speech of rain.

Suppose that, silent, clean of joy or pain,
leaves know more than we know of them; suppose
from root to bud something half-sentient flows
that dreams its drama too, poised on our sill,
imagining that fate—or what you will—
turns tables on them by design, to test
which of them perseveres, which endures best
journeys through changing light, bewildering rooms,
to hold some purpose high until it blooms.

Squirrel

Look how those smallest fingers clasp together
under the feeder swinging overhead,
how he yearns upward, flicks his grizzled feather
of tail, measuring those leaps that led
him to this cold sill, calculating how
to defy wet sleet and gravity, straight up
our window screen—and there he scurries now—
to bury his gray snout in that full cup.
He robs the chickadees, of course, he keeps
away what we intend to feed, and spatters
more than he eats into untidy heaps
that later sprout among the stones. Grave matters,
more than whether or not heaven is fair,
entirely deaf or not to such small prayer.

Leaving the Bittersweet

Vines so deep-rooted they outwit the frost
illuminate this page, the garden's text
of dormant shrubs whose script of twigs, crisscrossed
against each other and the sky, seems vexed
and jeweled by coils of red and saffron flowers.
Look how trees wear, along their blackened trunks,
rubrics of bloom, as in some Book of Hours
winter borrows the fantasies of monks.
Duty would have it gone, would pull it out
again, again, to keep the garden bare
in its bare season; but whose hand can rout
what rises from the dark to bless the air,
whatever Word such blossoming would mar?
Or can one follow metaphor too far?

All Saints' Day

Our maple has been sulking in the sun
three mortal days of fury without sound,
straining to pace and pose, alas, not one
inch from where water shackles it to ground.
Spoiled, spendrift, witless child who's somehow missed
the signal from last warning to this chill
close of accounts, it hurls from every fist,
as if to spurn the giver, each worn bill
crumpled to brown and scattered on dry grass.
Domestic drama, yes; but not to fear,
I've seen the maple come to grace, and pass
from scarlet impotence, by end of year,
into such white acceptance as to earn
peace better than redemption or return.

Guidelines

Here's what you need to do, since time began:
find something—diamond-rare or carbon-cheap,
it's all the same—and love it all you can.

It should be something close—a field, a man,
a line of verse, a mouth, a child asleep—
that feels like the world's heart since time began.

Don't measure much or lay things out or scan;
don't save yourself for later, you won't keep;
spend yourself now on loving all you can.

It's going to hurt. That was the risk you ran
with your first breath; you knew the price was steep,
that loss is what there is, since time began

subtracting from your balance. That's the plan,
too late to quibble now, you're in too deep.
Just love what you still have, while you still can.

Don't count on schemes, it's far too short a span
from the first sowing till they come to reap.
One way alone to count, since time began:
love something, love it hard, now, while you can.

Marine Salvage Museum, Florida

Artfully scattered, rings, filigree, chain,
in sand meant to suggest the ocean floor
that cradled the lost galleon, far from Spain;
look at this helmet some young noble wore
who wore the contents out nodding assent
to every sea-change since; note that rich urn
now sealed with coral. What this wreckage meant
to eyes beseeching God for its return
we only guess. Of course, if we had eyes
like God's, we could see all the scenes forthwith:
the keel still crowned with birds, its green disguise
intact; gold still unhammed by the smith;
the lady hanging on the handsome neck;
four centuries of tides scouring the deck.

In the Diner

The afternoon yawned empty as a plate:
he wasn't there. She settled down to wait.
She heard three voices in a neighboring booth
exchanging various versions of the truth
about some man—a neighbor—and his wife,
or lover, maybe. *Leads him a dog's life:*
humiliations, scenes; she likes to sleep
with his close friends; he doesn't make a peep,
said One. *And serves him right,* said Two.
He eats it up, said Three, *they always do.*
Haven't you noticed it's the steely bitches
who get their hooks in deepest? Don't know which is
first, her itch to hurt or his to be
hurt. Either way, they're suited to a T.

They tossed it back and forth, finished the pie,
waved napkins at the waitress, caught her eye,
ran quickly down the check and split it even.
Let's go, said One; *What kind of tip we leavin'?*
They rose and turned, flicked Danish from tight jeans
not meant for solid women past their teens.

Not quite the Fates, she thought, with life and death
skeined in their hands, not tempters of Macbeth
coaxing plot out of character. But still,
they left questions behind, as strangers will
whose passing words, half-heard and all unsought,
feed on what lives unworded in our thought.

How must it feel to be the one for whom
all else is lost? whose presence in a room

is flame and magnet both? the one who leaves
clawmarks—she wondered—to whom memory cleaves
because pain is adhesion, of a sort?
who thinks of love as game or as blood sport?

She thought of going: let him find her gone,
for once; but settled down and waited on.
She checked her watch: now he was very late.
Her life was plain before her on the plate.

As She Tells It

It's not those early days I best remember,
our first unworded oneness in the clearing
prepared for us, the wound in his side that closed
after God drew me out of him, the sword
sealing as it divided, the sweet recalcitrant
pull of him afterward that always

felt like a return. The earth was always
home in those days; both of us remember
how easily soil opened, unrecalcitrant,
inventing the green flavors of the clearing
for our delight. We hardly noticed the sword
in the angel's hand, or how the gates were closed.

I don't know when it was that something closed
between us, or why: I could not always
run to God's call, as he did, to the sword
of power sheathed in the voice I still remember.
He went willing and joyful to the clearing,
worked it to order; but I, recalcitrant

with questions, brooding doubts, recalcitrant
to law and season even as they bound me, closed
the core of me for good: thought was my clearing.
He named everything made, but did not always
find things behind their names, ceased to remember
the words we were forbidden by the sword.

Like things, we had been made; we had no sword;
we played like children, learned, recalcitrant
as buried stones, those rules we kept: remember

this, beware of that. The gates were closed,
the woods outside them dark, searchlights always
combing the sky, the borders of our clearing

towered and sentried. The end of it—the *clearing
of his good name,* as Adam called the sword
of his confession and betrayal—his always
unforgivable forgiveness, my recalcitrant
pride because I did the thing that closed
that brief first chapter—that's what I remember:

mind clearing itself free, recalcitrant
words learning to be a sword, the garden closed,
the dark always ours, deeper than we remember.

In Sioux Falls at Thirty-Seven

Last night I stood in your home town
and wondered on what quiet street
you practiced pitching as a boy,
or kicked loose pebbles with your feet.

On either hand, and flatter than
the pages of an open book,
lie miles of grass heavy with sun.
I take the road you never took,

unruffled as the sleeping fields.
No longer I, no longer you,
we meet in memories that seem
the dreams of people I once knew.

Who would be young again? Not I;
the skin's too thin at seventeen.
It takes this long to count as joy
the mercy of the years between!

Poem in April

Still, sober heart that kept me whole in youth,
be sober now, and guarded, and beware
those whispers in the wind that hush the truth.

Blossoms in their green mail, flags in the air,
crocuses in bright helmets through the snow,
all say *believe, believe*—but let them go:
this war is not for winning, not for you.
Better be still and guarded and not care
more for this budding branch than for the bare.
The hand that drew it bare composed this too,
and signed his work—this cheek, this frosty head.

Heart, you are not renewable; be wise.
Memory and desire, the poet said:
be sober, heart, the wind is full of lies.

If There Had Been

If there had been more time; if you had stayed;
if you had spoken sooner or said less;
if you had turned away; if the parade
had halted elsewhere; if the wrong address
had not been scribbled, or the train delayed;
if you had practiced prudence—or excess—
or practiced nothing but the play of chance;
if mind; if stubborn will; if circumstance;
if changes were new turns the gods allow;
if you had never been, or been before,
or were to come, or then not then but now;
if you had known that there would be no more
after this once; if you had guessed somehow;
if days were diamonds in a ring you wore.

Fractals

I overheard two speaking in the night:

What if, she said, *I have imagined quite*
all that there is of you, and nothing's here
by morning—not a lip, a lash, an ear—
to say I did not dream you?
                              Oh, well, then,
he laughed, *you'd have to summon me again,*
wouldn't you, wish by wish and bone by bone?

But no, she said, in the half-angry tone
in which a child who wants to be proved wrong
insists on an old fear. *What if I long*
for you to be, to be this that you are,
but what I've made you from is out there, far
as stars, or colors that my eyes can't know,
so that I only think I think you so?

I knew, as with some sense behind these five,
how he caressed her then, as if to drive
thought's demons from her flesh and wrestle doubt
with the one argument that shuts it out.

You may be my chimaera too, for all
I know, he said, *but let's agree to call*
each other by what names we can, for now.

And that was all I heard, but marveled how
certainty, which eludes us when we seek
in reason's name, will come for love, and speak
as for some kindly sleeper dreaming me,
who dreamt those sleepers and their reverie.

Contingencies

As if it mattered: still, you probe to trace
precisely when it was fate took and tossed
and overwhelmed you, find the very place
it was you stood on when you found—or lost—
the thing that mattered. When the envelope
slid through the slot, innocent as a stone;
what you were scrubbing when you wiped the soap
hastily on your apron, took the phone
and left the water running, out of breath
with interruptions, slow to grasp the news:
the baby's birthweight, say, or time of death,
or diagnosis, casual as a fuse;
or in some public room, the stranger's name
half-heard, and nothing afterward the same.

Canción Penúltima

Ave de trino mortal
que vuelas de beso en beso,
Dónde irás cuando naufrage
tu nido de carne y hueso?

Arpa de cinco cuerdas
que elogias la luz prestada,
Qué mano te hará caricias
cuando caigas en la nada?

Ay los ocasos de cobre,
mar de acero y hojalata,
ay luna que va sangrando
sus pesadumbres de plata!

Ay arces medio vestidos
de bronce, de azufre y grana,
lenguas de fuego que cantan
y no han de cantar mañana!

Next-to-last Song

Singer of mortal songs
in flight from kissing to kissing,
where shall you go when your nest
made of flesh and bone is missing?

Harp of five strings that play
in praise of this borrowed light,
what hand will caress you then,
fallen to endless night?

Oh setting of copper suns,
ocean of steel and tin,
oh moon that goes grieving by,
bleeding a silver skin!

Oh maples half dressed in bronze,
sulphur, scarlet in the wood,
tongues of flame that sing today,
tomorrow silent for good!

Hoy Me Pregunto

Hoy me pregunto—cosas de la edad—
quién me recordará cuando no esté,
y cómo. Así se busca una verdad
en libro y mano ajena, y se lee,
quizás, "Fue suave y tonta; inofensiva,
sí, pero esclava de impulsos." O, "Su don
de mirar verdadero, a carne viva,
cuando el sentir le permitía razón …"
etcetera. Qué hacer, si uno lo escrito
en ese tomo no lo ha de saber
ni revisar, sea vera historia o mito.
Mejor así, mejor que la mujer
viva, la tonta de hoy; y más allá,
que diga lo que diga quién dirá.

Lately I've Wondered

Lately I've wondered—it's a trick of age—
who will remember me some day, and how,
as one may strain one's eyes to glimpse a page
over another's shoulder, catching now
the words, … *soft, silly woman, not unkind*
but moved to rashness by the moment … ; then
later, … *gift for thought she was inclined*
to blunt with sentiment time and again.
But it's no use, what may be printed there
is not for me to phrase, not mine to know
or edit with vain wish; if not past care,
then past amending. Yes, and better so:
better the silly woman real today,
let him who will remember what he may.

Cleaning Out

What will they make of this detritus, they,
my judges in the future? Will they say,
Our great-great-grandmother preserved each snippet
for us to find her in, or will they tip it
into the trash without a word or glance?
Here's half a theater ticket tucked by chance
into a letter—cursive decades old—
whose paragraphs of gossip richly told
give evidence that someone once lived here
who bore my name. And this from you, my dear,
not proof against oblivion, but well meant
not quite to halt, but slow, at least, descent.
I ought to learn from leaves, accept the fall
they take with grace—paper or maple, all
easy, uncomplaining—toss away
these parachutes I keep. But not today.

At the Nurses' Station

Here's Rita, ninety-something, in red socks,
shuffling splay-footed up and down the ward,
pausing to turn a knob—there are no locks—
or detour round a wheelchair. She's a card,
brightens the shift fussing that it's so late
and she not home; complains her mother
must wonder why she's tarried; what a state
her family must be in! And another
complaint: her shoes are gone—stolen, no doubt.
Poor lady, goaded by the dead, not free,
trapped with the living and no short way out!
Or maybe lucky, after all, to be
so sure of home, so confident that they
who loved her once watch for her night and day.

Triptych

I. Departures

A woman grips her ticket; gate fourteen;
lines lumbering to board; holiday crowd
dressed for the islands, and a few who lean
idly before bright souvenirs and loud
paperbacks dressed for teasing. She is all
in black—tights, sweater, boots—as if to claim
new widowhood; but no, the only pall
she has borne lately is her father's name,
recently traded for another. There
they stand, waving, father, mother, groom,
herself, divided by the glass, each pair
smiling, moving away. She wonders whom
she is least wary of. And now they're next.
She tries to understand why she is vexed.

II. Suppose

A woman with a suitcase boards a bus.
She has shrugged off her life like a worn dress,
stepped clear of it, packed nothing to discuss
or mourn for; to be glad of, even less.
Solicitations, greetings, pile unread
below the slot; that wedding gift, unsent,
and those back issues scattered on the bed
(unmade, for once) must wonder where she went.
Another mile or two and daylight fails
where the bus sighs and lunges, and she sees—
just barely—endless stubble fields and rails.
There in the suitcase tucked between her knees
(still tagged with names she will not wear again)
nothing but a blank notebook and a pen.

III. Road Map

A woman spreads a road map on the seat,
fevered with purpose, bruised by what he said,
by what she shouted back. The mapled street
unspools behind her. Oh, the weeping bed
she stole downstairs from before dawn, that last
hard angry love made there, those silent fronts
of neighbors' porches watching her, aghast:
her daring, her departure! And at once—
hands trembling on the wheel, stricken, sweat cold
with fear of what she craves—foresees return,
rehearses how the road loops round to fold
back into what will have her, learns to learn
her name again, her place in these designs,
snug in her grief as in these fourteen lines.

Blue Valise

My blue valise left standing by the track
recedes with distance as we pick up speed
and disappears at last. I call it back,

but magic never works. There goes my stack
of notes, addresses I was sure I'd need,
in that valise left standing by the track,

lone, enigmatic. All night long to crack
of dawn, will passing strangers, as they lead
their cranky children home, pause to look back

at that Rosetta Stone whose stubborn lack
of human context makes it hard to read?
I've left my blue valise beside the track,

and not on purpose, though I have a knack
for scattering myself, as bead by bead
a broken necklace pours down breast and back

as if some grip had chosen to go slack
and willed the metaphor, if not the deed.
My blue valise is standing by the track.
I wish I could be sure I want it back.

Body's Weight

… The soul is the heart
without the body's weight; mine joins the others
hovering like angels.
　　　　　—*"Notice," Ma and Other Poems,*
　　　　　Morty Sklar

But body's weight is all there is to link
one to another; who would know, without
that shared encumbrance, when to turn and doubt
what the soul says to think?

I am afraid of those whose one desire
is unencumbered soul, those who believe
grace is a flair for lightness saints achieve
emerging from the fire.

Spare me soul's hard perfections; let the hands
of surgeons—lovers, too—learn to revere
and memorize what soul cannot hold dear
but body understands.

Let there be anaesthesia and fresh bread,
warm clothes in winter, and in summer, shade,
and let the saints forgive us what we weighed
as we forgive our dead.

Entropy

First, spinning wobbly,
the blurred coin clears, staggering down to flat;
the hurled stone slowing like an afterthought
collects itself earthward.

Then apples, past ripe,
cave to small rueful brown grins in their dish,
forgotten. And now a glad weariness
gives, like a door ajar

for some secret guest
complied with in silence; each vertebra
scrapes at its mealy socket; old orbits
decay with use, like nerves.

In Eight Degrees

In eight degrees last night the heater failed
where our plants court the sun. By morning light,
a scene of frosty carnage: spindly-tailed
spider plants dangling stiffly, their once-bright
little green gloves now pale as victim's hands;
begonias trailing red, disheveled hair
over and round clay pots, down iron stands
clear to the floor, in comical despair.
A faulty circuit-breaker, so I'm told,
not on the job—whatever that may be—
left these mute lives defenseless in the cold.
I picture nerves shut down, an artery
distended and untidy with the sludge
dumped by mistake or left to clot inside,
because some mindless molecule won't budge
until the thing it doesn't know has died.
Well, that's routine, and more of it to come.
For living things, courting the sun entails
nothing but risk, since, dumb or not-so-dumb,
sooner or later something always fails.

Kinderszenen

… When I was twelve, I still believed in God
And credited His Holy See …
                        —Len Krisak

There have been those God did not wholly see:
that boy, for one, charred in the hotel bed
his father fled before he lit the flame;
God let him live; interviewed on TV
in what gnarled flesh they patched him with, he said
he has no father. One who played a game
in a lush field alone tipped the brass frame
of an old cesspool seal; her childhood sped
swift as Persephone's to feed the ground
from which the harvest springs. And God played dead,
or was—or never was, says History.
But I say any father of the drowned,
the burned, the starved, the gassed, be named and found
until pity and shame have made Him be.

Case Study

I know a woman whose one son went bad,
stole cash out of her purse, hunted and found
her wedding ring and sold it; all she had
he concentrated on a band around
his arm, a needle in his vein. And she,
who mopped an office building floor by floor
all night to keep him safe as he could be,
blames all her life on "life"—on being poor,
on giving birth too young, on the young love
who left her, the malevolence of stars
she pictures at their conclave high above
her, plotting what to frustrate, what to mar
to shape the constellations of her grief—
but never blames her son, who died a thief.

Crab Poem

Consider Mr. Crab, who after his
brief tenancy with us, saw fit to crawl
out of the tepid comfort of his tank
into our den, out of his life's show biz
low comedy to his lone Grand Guignol.
Time was, after tapdancing up a bank
of leafy green, he'd take a curtain call,
one rosy claw flourished in jaunty thanks.
Now, on our knees, we search corner and crack.
Not easy, this belief that sparrows fall,
that harmless clowns blunder toward doom like this,
while heaven sees and opts to turn its back
rather than shut a gate or switch a track
or whisper in some ear, *Look, there he is!*

Exercise

Stopper your ears and the sluices of the heart
deafen you with the wash and rush of blood
obsessing, outward and back, outward and back.

Finger the pulse at your throat, or at the blue
deltas of wrist or ankle, or the elbow's
crease of crushed silk, and the hushed pounding

invites you in, teaches you what you're made of
and how it falters, what the tremor says,
and the whisper: How to work in this noise!

But spread your fingers on this winter window
instead, and the body's sudden silence
fills with the fuss of sparrows, patter of flakes

on glass, old leaves under hedges gathered
for revision by rain and roots plotting
versions of summer you need not edit.

Three for the Bones

I. Trick or Treat

I know you're in there, with your ear-to-ear-
wide laugh at our expense framed by the black
hood of that cape, though you're just passing through
this time, making the rounds, closing the year
with droll reminders, candy in your sack
like tribute to a king. But this is you,
I know; in jovial mood, but genuine: who
else, tricked out by pumpkin-light, a pack
of clownish, noisy beasts all scaled and furred
behind your shouldered scythe, has such a knack
for banter and suspense, for rousing fear
that grips the throat, for making fear absurd?
Yes: in that childish pleading threat, I heard,
I heard, I know it's you, I know you're here.

II. Tenant

And here, in the hard crater round each eye
my fingers find you, in the hinge of jaw,
ladder of spine. You are the tenant of
this house called by my name, recluse so shy
you hide from daylight. No one ever saw
you living but the surgeon, mask and glove
bent to unsheathe you, with his kind of love,
from your intimate garment of red raw
silk. The love we know prefers this dress,
this downy coat for stroking, fingered paw,
moist human muzzle warm until we die.
And then you're all there is, both more and less
than what you were, tenant and master, yes,
but nameless and indifferent and bone-dry.

III. Parable

Bone-dry and winter-gray, without a sound
the garden sleeps; now all the chambers close
where life endures. By spring—who can believe
that word will ever come?—from each small mound
as from a vault, alyssum and moss rose
thread their blind passage out of darkness, cleave
the soil and bloom. But first they must conceive
of sun, give themselves to what faith knows,
as once that girl the angel called from prayer
conceived of god, or so her story goes.
Rise, every sleeping thing: look to be found
useful by the least brightness in the air;
be trowel to rouse the sod, trellis to bear
the weight of what we know stirs in the ground.

Dinner, Ocala, February 1997

Laughing long over dinner with good friends,
pouring old stories priceless as old wine
freely as water, we become aware
of changes in the light: how night contends
with sun about the trees, and draws a line
of shadows down the gold-and-dusty air
to penetrate this quiet room now, where
we summon back four decades as we dine:
how some are gone, how others fated never
to laugh with us again still send a sign
to say they hear us; how our laughter mends
this thread more rapidly than loss can sever
an inch of it; how good is good forever,
untouched by when it goes or how it ends.

Lily of the Valley

Down on my knees to clear away what's lost,
I track them by their fragrance first, and then
fall into their green ambush, find the frost
of their unlikely bivouac again
under the blackened leaves of winter kill.
Who would have held out hope for them, so much
around them ravaged, brought to nil
by small degrees, long nights, January's touch!
Blessed be all that lives to come unbidden
to our astonished love—the bloom, the child,
each serendipitous joy that springs half hidden
from last year's death, this human gift for wild
surprised retrieval out of less and less,
this gift of tongues that teaches us to bless.

Exploratory

The young technician warns me, with regret,
You're going to feel this just a bit, OK?
She uses her gloved hand deftly, to set
my chin, my arm, my breast. The first x-ray
shows the troublesome nodule that she needs
to train the lens on like some inner Mars;
now, pain—a silent siren—while she reads
my body's horoscope in its own stars.
What shall I call this planet in my space
spinning its narrow orbit through live flesh?
But no, a false alarm, a gift, a grace-
period to count my blessings, start afresh.
Get dressed, she says, *we'll check it in six months.*
I've made it back into my life, this once.

Leonardo's Metaphor

The body, in Leonardo's metaphor,
was an organ on which the soul played.
　　　　—Milton Kirchman, *Leonardo da*
　　　　Vinci on Creative Processes in Art

No, not huge pipes ranked like a marching band,
plural and public, decked with gilded strips
like epaulets. More like something the hand
caresses as it learns to play, the lips
shaping themselves around some private joy:
flute, maybe, shepherd's pipe. Or better still,
harmonica: let soul be like some boy
idle, for once, perched on a modest hill
that overlooks his father's farm, small streams
skirting familiar fields, and over there
those other fields he knows only in dreams
where he imagines colors, tastes the air
for smoke and mint, discovers bark and stone,
breathes himself into music, moan on moan.

On The Ambivalence of Angels:
Expulsion from Paradise, Giovanni di Paolo

In this Expulsion scene, for instance, where
our youthful parents exit on the right,
a winged adolescent steers the pair
over the lost millefleurs of their delight
with half a smile, one hand on Adam's shoulder.
Behind him, a plate inscribed with grief:
cracked hills where they must labor and grow older
to be each other's torment and relief,
freedom their single weapon. As they turn,
blind to the pointing deity in blue,
who scowls, see how the angel seems to yearn
after them, as if eager to come too,
clear of the gold circling his head about,
into this life he's heard he's blessed without.

The Ball Game: Chichén Itzá

The winner—not the loser, says our guide—
gave himself willingly to the obsidian
blade. Look, this is how he died,
kneeling, exuberant, seven vermilion
serpentine arrows of his young blood flying
up from the severed neck. He has, it seems,
not yet become aware of his own dying,
but slipped clean past it to some realm of dreams
to join the gods he chose, who've chosen him.
Clearly he felt their purpose in the game,
clearly he saw them through this lacy scrim
of stone incised to praise each one by name.
See the stone hoop through which he made the toss
that earned him his bright version of the cross.

Tapestry

A shallow forest spangled with millefleurs;
a horse, head down, grazing the noonday shade;
a knight, morose with duty. Nothing stirs
except perhaps one raven, and a maid
cramped by the window of her tiny tower
an inch or two away, under gold eaves,
wimpled in white, holding a single flower,
her grief contained by a fine lace of leaves.
The horse would turn and take familiar roads
back, but the rider's on a quest that leads
him on beyond the tasseled frame, and goads
master and mount alike, although one needs
nothing but grass to crop, and one will find
nothing to want but what he left behind.

Pentimento

*Vermeer had evidently attempted to paint out
a figure, and traces of this form are still visible
beside the two women chatting in the foreground.*
　　　—Sir Herbert Read: *The Great
Artists, Book 19*

I am the curious absence that your eye
can almost see through, here and yet not here,
excised from Delft, its huge and placid sky,
its shallow stream, by God, alias Vermeer.
Why he first made, then banished me away—
leaving this faintest pigment like a soul
to mark me gone—is more than I can say.
Maybe he found me wanting, not as whole
as these two women, or those other few
gathered beside the boat, set to depart;
maybe he worked in grief, because he knew
himself the secret flaw that marred his art.
Think of me as the smudge on this near shore
for which your life is one brief metaphor.

Paul Helleu Sketching with His Wife,
John Singer Sargent

This is the woman Marcel Proust would find
most tedious, the painter's pretty wife,
Madame Helleu—relaxed or bored?—reclined,
looking beyond the canvas, as if life
were there outside the frame. Inside, soft light,
almost impartial on their hats, the boat,
his pallete, brushes, fishing pole upright
against his sketch, settles upon his coat
sleeve—one in color with the marshy grass—
and on his fingers poised in rapt midstroke.
If we could enter this caught moment, pass
beyond their silence to what words they spoke,
we should know better why he loved her so.
Assuming there are reasons one can know.

Portrait of Don Manuel Osorio de Zúñiga

Note how those birds beside him, in the cage
near his white slippers rich with satin bows,
trust in their master and do not engage
the three rapt cats, one with a look that glows
out of black fur and blackness of intent,
one gazing out beyond the gilded frame,
and one, all appetite but impotent,
at the pet mockingbird that drops a name—
Francisco Goya—from his beak before
the youthful patron, Don Manuel. A string
links child and bird and painter's signature,
as if to say that genius, claw and wing
must share alike the favor of the small
red velvet connoisseur who owns them all.

Nothing New

The paintings of Corot are beautiful,
but reveal nothing new.
                    —Jean Francois Millet, August 22,
                        1865

Corot, in *Souvenir of Montfontaine,*
enshrines the landscape, yes, but tells the truth
as truth is told by memory, whose *then*
is flora salvaged by departure, youth
as it might have been but perhaps never
was nor should have been, oneself translated
from the crabbed speech of mind, the passing clever,
into heart's monosyllables. It's dated
eighteen-hundred-sixty-four: Bismarck,
Sherman, Ibsen, Jules Verne and Jean Valjean.
But the young woman straining though the dark
leafage to pluck a twig—she barely can—
wants only *this,* though why we cannot know,
before it falls away where such thing go.

Corot, *Man Scything by a Willow Plot*

A veritable cell of willow green,
willow cathedral, from whose nearly black
chapels of bark the sky is barely seen.
On the far right, a woman, whose shawled back
suggests a child carried on her left arm,
looks for the man to turn: she may have come
bearing his midday meal from the home farm,
or may be passing, going to or from
some neighbor's house. The worker at his task
of scything is thigh-deep in feathery
green, intent, turned inward, seems to ask
that nothing interrupt this reverie
in which his body and his work are one,
as she, in passing, wishes she had done.

On the Power of Love to Ennoble the Spirit

The Taj Mahal, for instance: how that king
conjured, by force of will and others' hands,
towers like songs for one beloved thing
lost; how his perfect offering still stands,
unequaled; how the flame of such devotion
tempers and purifies, refines to gold
the dust one man is made of, lifts emotion
above mere passing grief. And I've been told
that widowed king, both passionate and wise,
severed his workmen's hands, the clever head
of his chief architects, plucked out the eyes
of draftsmen, so to honor his dear dead
queen with the last, the crowning, gift of men
who would not build its like ever again.

The Bath, Mary Cassatt

Mother and child, confined, seen from above
within strong patterns: carpet, papered wall,
the woman's robe striped green and white and mauve.
Dark heads together, their two glances fall
together also on the bowl of water—
warm, certainly, rimmed lavender and gold—
in which the mother's hand cradles the daughter's
foot, a gesture that the three-year-old
consents to grudgingly. The child's right hand
echoes the mother's, on her own plump thigh,
and there on Mama's knee, her left, in bland
acceptance, rests. One wonders what the eye
of the skilled artist made of this other life,
she who was never mother, never wife.

Translating

This is an art difficult as marriage
whose medium is the stony grit of language
that rends—and renders—message from mirage.

Not the clear eye of love that reads, if briefly,
all there may be and wills to fasten bravely
on what is not, choosing to find it lovely;

no, this is harder, this is love in action,
not contemplation; this is live dissection
cobbling the monster into breathing fiction,

discarding this, salvaging that. One wish:
synchronous motion like those parts that thrash
in porno flicks to be not quite one flesh;

and one fruition: how the face, the phrase,
through long devotion manages to fuse—
not sum, not seamless—into compromise

that's neither old nor wholly new, but rather
echo dopplering off, off by a feather,
but circling back, miraculous, together.

On Hearing My Name Pronounced Correctly, Unexpectedly, for Once

The voice over the wire trills my R,
snares me with soft diminutives, and waits
for me, in our shared language, to allow
my words to trace, like fingers down a scar,
stories we've known since childhood, places, dates
in brackets on worn stones. He tells me how
our old ones slip away, forgetting, now,
faces and names. My cousin hesitates;
I take this name again and say goodnight.
Odd how the gringo tongue that shifts, translates
you into something it can say, but far
from what you were, that never gets you right,
rolling you round too long, too smooth, too light,
loves you at last to who it says you are.

The Poet's Husband Engages
in Gourmet Cooking

My better half, who's in the kitchen,
has summoned me—again—to pitch in,
clear out the sink, take down two bowls.
He's proud he can reverse our roles,
nurture his skill for fancy cooking.
I wish he'd nurture skill at looking—
no, better still—genius for finding
where things are kept, without reminding;
for wiping, sweeping, washing, drying,
removing grease from earlier frying.
But no, in half an hour twelve times
I'm called from soon-forgotten rhymes,
from perfect metaphors chewed up,
to point out pan and eight-ounce cup
and colander there on their hooks,
where one may find them, if one looks.
At times like these, one's thoughts embark
on reveries forbidden, dark,
whose very joy invites distress:
the phrase *No Forwarding Address,*
life in some distant not-quite-hovel
with someone working on his novel
wholly immersed in Chapter Three,
living on cake and cheese, like me.

Item

Escaped: one poem,
winged, half worded,
too soon flowered,
starred and birded,

simile'd
and metaphored.
Warning: author
badly gored.

Cornered, poem
will spring to bite.
No threatening moves,
no sudden light;

keep your distance;
stay behind it.
Call this number
if you find it.

She Resists, but Barely

Look at the state of wild undress you've caught
me in, Poem, lying about, with all
the housework still untouched! God knows I've fought
you—but how hard? Or did I mean to fall,
and leave my thoughts unclothed, indolent, out
of guile, my mind unlocked, so you could slip
right in and find me? That's what you're about,
I know: seduction, your insidious lip
pressed to my ear. I ought to sew and cook;
I ought to sweep and wash; I ought to dust.
But you have stirred my dust instead, and look
how duty yields to my peculiar lust,
your silky promise of some further bliss,
and not a thing to cover me but this.

Workshop

We're in your poem, a large rumpled bed
in a cramped room; full ashtrays, underwear,
one window, sooty, small; above my head,
a dingy fixture; little clumps of hair
gathering underfoot. Advice, you say,
is what you want. Though I'm not sure you mean it,
here goes: Vacuum, do laundry, cart away
those furry dishes. Then, *after* you clean it,
make the room say your life, as if it wanted
to keep your life a secret, but must tell
despite itself; as if the bed were haunted
by what you dreamt in it, by what befell
the dreamer of that dream, by what it knew.
How to perform such feats? That's up to you.

On the Walls

From the first look I knew he was no good.
That perfumed hair, those teeth, those smiling lips
all said, *Come home with me.* I knew I would.

Love? Who can say? Daylight withdrew in strips
along those vaulted archways waiting where
the slaves would hear us whisper on the stair.
Not smart, not interesting—no, not the best
at anything, all talk and fingertips.
The best I left behind; they're in those ships
nosing your harbor. You can guess the rest.
The heart does what it does, and done is done.

Regret? What for? The future finds its Troys
in every Sparta, and your fate was spun
not by old crones, but pretty girls and boys.

Vignette

Andromache, one misty morning,
walking the city's crown of stones,
is startled by a cry whose warning
pierces the marrow of her bones.

The child beneath her heart is stirred,
turns in its groove as if to know
what augury without a word
intrudes where such calm waters flow.

The sentry, stolid at his post,
salutes Prince Hector's pretty wife.
He cannot know how, ghost by ghost,
she has relinquished death for life.

He wonders why she reads this place
as if it were a graven prayer,
as if Scamander's cursive pace
inscribed the sum of blessings there.

How blessed—she thinks—*this plain, unhaunted,*
where those I cherished never bled;
blessed, to be ordinary, wanted
by the good man who shares my bed.

The mist has cleared; far off and pale,
the cry she heard takes form at last:
only a gull, circling a sail
approaching neither slow nor fast.

Quiet, Now

Quiet, now: the wind is reading a story,
riffling through green volumes of spruce and balsam,
unearthing fables from the runes of lichen,
elucidating parables of crows propped
open on the lectern of naked maples.

Patience: the wind is reading a long story
with miracles in it, rumors of the marsh
weeping for joy over the sky's reflection,
promise of resurrections, of pale crocus
lifting its crown from the wreckage of summer.

Skimming every field, uncovering old plots
on those white pages time writes on, the wind goes
where the snake waits in its hole, deaf as the heart
in its cage of longing. Be still now: listen:
the wind, the wind is reading you a story.

On the Impossibility of Translation

Of course impossible, transmuting touch
and color into sound, sound into sign,
sign into sense again and back: too much
struggling after the names for flavor, line,
knowing they can't be found, no, not in one
language: in two? across the grain of speech?
Unthinkable! Easier to fold the sun
into its syllable. Yet lovers, each
mute in one skin, can learn to speak in tongues,
speak themselves whole, if only once; you've heard,
fitful above the fields, the summer sung
in high, cascading turns of fluent Bird,
and seen, in shallow pools in every town,
how rain translates the sky and writes it down.

About the Author

Rhina P. Espaillat, born in the Dominican Republic in 1932, has lived in the U.S. since 1939 and taught English in New York City at the high school level. She has been writing since childhood, and has published seven full-length books and three chapbooks, comprising poetry, essays, and short stories in both English and her native Spanish. She has also published work in numerous anthologies and magazines, as well as translations, most notably of Robert Frost into Spanish and St. John of the Cross into English. Her awards include the T. S. Eliot Prize for Poetry, the Richard Wilbur Award, the Nemerov Prize, the May Sarton Award, and several from the Poetry Society of America, the New England Poetry Club, and the Ministry of Culture of the Dominican Republic.

She lives in Newburyport, Massachusetts, where she and her husband, sculptor Alfred Moskowitz, are active in the arts organizations of the community. One of her goals is lowering barriers between the cultures she considers herself part of, and encouraging the art of translation and literary exchange, especially among students and young people of many backgrounds.